BEING
APT TO TEACH
AND HOLDING
THE MYSTERY
OF THE
FAITH

WITNESS LEE

Living Stream Ministry
Anaheim, California

© 2002 Living Stream Ministry

First Edition, March 2002.

ISBN 0-7363-1690-6

Published by

Living Stream Ministry
2431 W. La Palma Ave., Anaheim, CA 92801 U.S.A.
P. O. Box 2121, Anaheim, CA 92814 U.S.A.

Printed in the United States of America

02 03 04 05 06 07 08 / 10 9 8 7 6 5 4 3 2 1

CONTENTS

PREFACE

This book is composed of messages given in Chinese by Brother Witness Lee in Taipei, Taiwan in 1951. Its seven chapters elucidate the true meaning of being apt to teach and of holding the mystery of the faith. They also cover a few matters concerning service, such as how to discuss church affairs, how to care for the newly saved ones, and how to receive the believers.

Chapter One

BEING APT TO TEACH
AND HOLDING THE MYSTERY

TWO ASPECTS OF SPIRITUAL LEARNING

First Timothy 3:2 says that overseers must be "without reproach" and "apt to teach," and verse 9 says that deacons must hold "the mystery of the faith in a pure conscience." Then 2 Corinthians 4:1-2 says, "Therefore having this ministry as we have been shown mercy, we do not lose heart;...not walking in craftiness nor adulterating the word of God, but by the manifestation of the truth commending ourselves to every conscience of men before God." These verses show that if a person desires to minister to others spiritually as an overseer, a deacon, or an apostle, he needs to have some spiritual learning.

Being Apt to Teach—
the Experience of Spiritual Life

This learning has two aspects. The first is the aspect of spiritual experience—being apt to teach; the second is the aspect of the mystery of the truth—holding the mystery of the faith. One aspect is the experience, and the other aspect is the truth. If someone who serves the Lord desires to minister to others in a practical way in the service, he must have some spiritual experience. Our capacity, ability, and intelligence cannot enable us to serve properly. They cannot bring forth the living and service needed in the church. Although society depends on human capacity, ability, and intelligence, the church needs those who can supply life to others in spirit, and the amount and weight of the life one can supply altogether depends upon the measure of one's spiritual life.

Spiritual Experiences
Supplying the Spiritual Life in Reality

A newly saved one can also supply life to others. The life he supplies, however, is relatively immature. If the apostle Paul were to come into our midst and minister life to us, the life he would minister would surely be rich and weighty because he was a person with experience. The reason we cannot minister life richly to others is because what we have as our inner content is too immature. We should not only supply life to others, but we should also pay attention to the content of our supply. The content of our supply depends upon our spiritual experience. If we merely minister to others the spiritual knowledge that is in our mind, then what we minister will be merely doctrine and not life. Since doctrine is merely doctrine, it cannot supply life in reality.

For instance, perhaps you have recently prayed much and have also been in thorough fellowship with the saints. As a result, when people come in contact with you, they will be able to sense your freshness and receive your supply. It is quite possible that because your spirit is joyful, fresh, and lively, you will be able to stir people up whenever you contact them. However, if you could go further and minister the life in you to others through your contact with them, then they would also receive something real into them. Instead of merely being stirred up in their feelings, they would receive spiritual reality. Causing people to feel fresh and excited in their spirit is just a procedure and not the goal. Our goal is to give people the spiritual supply in reality.

Fanning the Spirits of Others into Flame
That They May Receive the Spiritual Supply

The reason we fan a person's spirit into flame is so that his closed, old, and deadened spirit may be lifted up and opened so that he can receive the spiritual supply in reality. What is the spiritual supply in reality? Let us consider the matter of consecration. Suppose that we have learned the lesson of consecration before the Lord in our daily living, and we not only know the meaning of consecration, but we also live in the reality of consecration. Consecration has become our living, our experience, our element, and our constitution. It is as if consecration is in our blood to the extent that it could be detected in us through analytical tests. Then one day we contact someone while we are in spirit and in fellowship with the Lord, and due to the freshness in our spirit, that person becomes stirred up and opens his stale, old spirit to receive the Lord. At this juncture, the Lord may give us the feeling that this person needs to know consecration. Therefore, we supply him with the reality of consecration in a good way. Thus, at that time consecration is not mere knowledge but is like a seed of life sown into him. A fresh, open spirit is like air, sunlight, and the soil that is ready for a seed to be planted in it.

Everyone knows that before a seed can be sown, the soil needs to be prepared. However, if there is sunlight, water, soil, and air but no seed, nothing will grow. Therefore, when we minister to others, we cannot just repeatedly cause them to feel refreshed within without planting something real into them. For this reason, in our daily life we must learn something of life and have spiritual experiences step by step. Only by doing this can we actively minister life in spirit to others. For example, consider the matter of consecration mentioned earlier. In our daily life we must have specific experiences of consecration by learning to put the world aside, to put away sins, to crucify the flesh with Christ, to submit to the breaking of the self, and to be restricted and disciplined in the Holy Spirit. Only in this way will we be those who truly live a life of consecration and who are able to minister the reality of consecration to others.

The Supply of Spiritual Reality Being Dependent on Our Learning and Experience in Our Daily Life

Without learning we will not have anything stored up within us, and without anything stored up within us, our inner content will not be rich. Thus, what we impart to others will be like air, like an empty packet that does not contain any seeds. After we visit someone, he may be somewhat excited inwardly, but there may not be anything growing in him. This is a very serious matter. We must see that our work is a work of sowing. After visiting someone five times, has the seed of life been sown into him? Have we merely given him "sunlight" and "air," or have we given him the most important thing—the seed of life? It is futile to give people sunlight, air, and water if we do not sow the seed of life into them. This is a serious matter, and we must be deeply impressed with it. It is not enough to be stirred up merely to pray. At most, this is just like having the right kind of environment—like the air that a seed needs in order to grow. However, we must also have the real seed of life. To have the real seed of life, we need to go before the Lord to learn and experience. We should not merely be excited and uplifted in spirit. Instead, we must have the reality of life sown into our spirit. We need to pursue matters such as dealing with sins, living before God, caring for the inner feeling, following the inward leading, and having fellowship and coordination in the Holy Spirit with the brothers and sisters. However, we cannot learn all these matters within a short period of time. We have to learn and experience them step by step.

We also need to help others while we are learning. We cannot engage merely in promoting and exhorting. Rather, we ourselves first have to learn a little, and then we can teach a little. The extent of our learning determines the extent of our teaching. On the one hand, what matters is not the extent of our learning but the spirit and reality; on the other hand, the more we learn, the more we will be able to supply. In any case, we absolutely must live before the Lord, paying attention to spiritual experience and not living merely in excitement or simply seeking to have the right "environment" within us. We must also have the seed, and how much real seed we have altogether depends on how much learning and experience we have in our daily life.

Being Able to Minister Life to Others
Only by Accepting the Death of the Cross

In the past when we spoke about the death of the cross, we

did not clearly see that to condemn and judge our problems is to accept the death of the cross. If we would learn to condemn and judge our problems daily, we would gain something real and spiritual. After gaining this spiritual reality, when we meet people with problems, we will be able to minister to these people what we have learned. Then what we give them will not only create the right environment within them, but it will be a life that is solid and able to help them. Otherwise, their flesh will still be the flesh, they will not have received life, and we will only be stirring up the proper environment within them. In other words, if we do not experience the breaking of the cross, then when we visit someone, there will be no change in his condition. He may be exposed to "sunlight," but no life will be added into him.

If a person has been broken by the cross in his natural disposition and is controlled and restricted by the Holy Spirit, then when he contacts people, spontaneously he will cause them to be restricted not only in their natural being but also in many other aspects. The lesson of being broken will be a real seed of life that can be planted into people's hearts as the field. However, this altogether depends upon his learning and dealings in his daily life. At present the majority of the work that most of us are doing is still the stirring up of the proper environment within people. This is not proper because it will not last long. We must have something that is of life to sow into people. If we do not take the opportunity to sow the seed of life into people while there is a good environment within them, then this good atmosphere might become a hindrance to them rather than a help. When this good environment passes away, they will become depressed and revert to their original condition. At that point, to stir up a proper environment within them again will no longer be useful. Therefore, although it is necessary to stir up the environment, we also must be prepared to sow the things of life into people after we do this.

For this reason we must look to the Lord that we would not just be excited for a moment but exercised every moment of every day. Whenever we have a feeling about a certain thing, we must deal with it before the Lord. We must have dealings not only concerning the meetings but also in all other matters. In every aspect of our daily walk we must correspond to the nature of God. This is what we need to learn before God. Then we can minister to others what we have learned.

Holding the Mystery—Understanding the Truth

Taking the Scriptures as the Basis and Principle in Everything

Furthermore, everyone who has a heart to learn to serve must understand the divine truths. He must read the Scriptures diligently, and in his reading he must seek out the basic principles in them. While reading the Scriptures, he must enter into the spiritual reality of the Scriptures and allow the Holy Spirit to enlighten him before God so that he may see the mystery of the faith. In this way he will become apt to teach. How can a person teach others if he does not know the mystery of the faith? He cannot. Therefore, everyone who has a heart to learn to minister to the church should pray a prayer similar to that of Solomon, saying, "O Lord, I am only a little child raised up by You. I do not know how to rule over the people. Lord, give me wisdom, not for myself but for You and for Your kingdom, that I may be able to discern between right and wrong" (cf. 1 Kings 3:7-9). Solomon's prayer was pleasing to the Lord, and because Solomon did not pray for longevity or wealth for himself, God answered his petition. If we all prayed this kind of prayer every day, then we would not despise the service of the church, and would not consider what we do to be less weighty than the work of a king. Then when the Lord returns, we will all see that what we were doing was much higher and weightier than what the kings on the earth were doing.

What we do today may affect hundreds and thousands of souls. Thus, it is quite possible that due to a small mistake in our judgment, someone might be weakened. If this happens, there is no telling how great the effect of it will be. It may be likened to throwing a stone into a lake, producing wave after wave of ripples. We do not know how far-reaching the effect will be.

We must not fall into a situation of being unable to administer the affairs of the church because we do not have sufficient light of the truth or adequate knowledge of the mystery of the truth, or because we are not clear concerning the principles in the Scriptures. We need to spend time to study the basic principles, not merely the teachings, in the holy Scriptures. We must do our best to determine these principles.

If we do this, then when we are about to make a decision concerning a certain matter, we will be less likely to make a mistake because we will know the basic principles. The responsible ones in the churches all have a burden upon them. The souls of thousands of people are hanging upon them. If they make a mistake, thousands of souls will be affected. Therefore, every time they make a decision or a judgment, they must not be careless. They need to have the insight of the faith. We are not establishing a nation with a constitution. We are shepherding the church by the Scriptures. This is not an easy thing to do. Today the reason we can stand firmly on the foundation of the truth and not be shaken by anyone is because we hold on to the intrinsic principles in the Scriptures. This pathway is not our creation or invention, for God has shown us the basic light of the revelations in the Scriptures. Regardless of how much we are opposed, we have these basic revelations as our solid ground.

The Lord said that if our work is not established upon His words, then it is like the house built upon the sand that fell when the rain descended, the rivers came, and the wind blew. If our work is established upon the Lord's words, then it is like the house built upon the rock which could not be destroyed by the water or wind (Matt. 7:24-27). Therefore, whenever we make a decision in the church, we must not be careless. Rather, we must have the Scriptures as the base.

Not Holding Merely the Faith
but the Mystery of the Faith

The portion of the Scriptures that we quoted at the

beginning of this chapter tells us to hold the mystery of the faith. It does not say that we should hold the faith but that we should hold the mystery of the faith. Some may consider head covering to be an item of the faith, but what is the mystery of this matter? The mystery is that we human beings should subject ourselves to God's authority. The covering of the sisters' heads represents our being in subjection to God's authority. God is our Head, and we are under Him. Let us consider the matter of baptism, which some may also consider to be an item of the faith. When we go into the water and come up again, this is not merely to keep the faith of baptism but even more to hold the mystery of the faith of baptism. The mystery is that in baptism we die with Christ, are buried with Him, and are raised together with Him, resulting in the Lord's life entering into us.

Today many people in Christian denominations and organizations hold only the faith but do not hold the mystery of the faith. Instead, some may take in the mystery of Satan. Therefore, everyone who serves in the church must understand the mystery of the faith. Otherwise, when he serves God's children, there is no telling where he will lead the saints. In regard to the sisters' head coverings, we should not merely advise the sisters on the selection of the style, color, and size of the head covering. Rather, we should serve them in a way that would bring them under the headship of Christ. In this way we are not merely holding the faith but holding the mystery of the faith. This requires us to have experiences in our daily life and to take the Bible and the principles contained in it as our foundation. On the one hand, we should have the experience, and on the other hand, we must have the biblical truths as the confirmation of our experience. Every one of us who serves the Lord must learn these two aspects.

Chapter Two

HOW TO DISCUSS
THE MATTERS OF THE CHURCH

When we encounter a difficult matter in our service in the church, how should we discuss it and make a decision concerning it? Should the matter be settled by one person's word, or should it be decided by everyone expressing his opinion and then taking a vote? Is the democratic way of deciding by the majority applicable in church service? In the Catholic Church only what the pope says matters whereas in the Protestant churches it is what the majority says that counts. Is there a place for these two methods in the Scriptures? Our simple and categorical answer is, "Absolutely not!" In the Bible there is absolutely no place for decisions to be made by one individual, and there is also no place for decisions to be made by the majority. Neither has a place in the Bible. Since this is the case, what is the way that matters are decided in the church life? From the human point of view, there seems to be only two ways—either the way of one individual making the decisions or the way of the majority making the decisions. In the Bible, however, we can see a third way.

THE HOLY SPIRIT OPERATING IN EVERYONE
TO BRING FORTH A DECISION

Although there is not much record in the Bible concerning the administration of the church, the elders and apostles in the early days of the church definitely followed certain principles of service in the administration of the church. Acts 15 gives us a pattern of how to manage and handle church affairs. In this chapter the problem in the church was resolved neither by the opinion of one individual nor by the opinion of the majority. Instead, it was resolved by the Holy Spirit's passing through and operating in the church. Therefore, decisions made in the church life should not reflect the opinion of a single individual acting in an autocratic way or an opinion that is derived from a democratic vote by everyone. Instead, the Holy Spirit operates in the church, and the church makes its decisions according to and along with the Holy Spirit.

By the Fellowship of the Elders of the Church Together with the Apostles

This kind of decision is reached not by the Holy Spirit alone but by the Holy Spirit passing through and operating in the church. In other words, when something happens, the matter is not decided by one person praying and having an angel appear to him to show him the right way. Neither is it decided by all the members praying until the Holy Spirit speaks forth the Lord's intention through someone as a prophet. All the decisions concerning the church should be decided in the following manner. When the church discovers that there is a problem that cannot be settled or resolved, then what to do in this situation should be decided not by just one person or by the opinion of the majority. Instead, all the apostles and all the elders—those who represent the church—should gather together. This group of people should include all the apostles and elders in that locality at that time.

Speaking to the Full Extent during the Fellowship

The elders represent the local church, and the apostles represent the churches in various localities. The elders represent one locality, and the apostles represent various localities. Just as the elders clearly understand the situation in a locality, so the apostles clearly understand the situations in various localities. When these two groups of people are put together, they understand the situation of all the saints in various places, and as a result they do not hold on to their own one-sided opinions. On the one hand, they are clear about the situation of the saints in various localities, and on the other hand, they do not insist on their own opinions. Instead, through fellowship they present what they understand and have observed concerning what God has done in the saints in various places. In this kind of fellowship everyone has the opportunity to speak, and they can speak as much as they like. This is the pattern shown to us in Acts. Everyone may speak to the full extent.

Not Being Fleshly in the Fellowship and Discussion

Sometimes in the meetings of the elders and co-workers, the majority of those in the meeting may not say anything, as if they have no opinions. After the meeting, however, one person may say one thing while another person may say another thing, and all their opinions come out. To not speak a single word during the meeting and then to speak many things and express all kinds of opinions after the meeting is a manifestation of the flesh. Such a person avoids speaking in the meeting in order to save his face, because he is afraid that he might not speak well. This is the flesh. However, since he is full of complaints in his heart, after the meeting he expresses an opinion about one matter and another opinion about another matter. This is also the flesh. We need to be delivered by God from caring for our face and personal feelings so that we may be open to speak, to fellowship, and even to debate according to the sense given to us by the Holy Spirit. We should try to learn how to debate with others in the church life without being fleshly. This is not easy to do.

Suppose after someone had just finished expressing an opinion, you were to immediately stand up and say, "Brother, I feel that what you have said is not accurate enough, and I feel that it should be this way." It would be quite difficult to say this and overturn his opinion without being in the flesh. In Acts there are two phrases which are very pleasant. One is *when much discussion had taken place* (15:7), and the other is *for it seemed good to the Holy Spirit and to us* (v. 28). It is abnormal to become so spiritual that it seems that the Holy Spirit is making all the decisions alone, without the "and to us"—without human beings coming together to discuss things.

We should be delivered from our flesh and come together to discuss matters without insisting on our own personal preferences. We should be able to consider a certain matter from different angles and discuss it from various angles. If we are able to do this, the Holy Spirit will be able to move freely among us. This is real discussion. For example, someone may say that the Gentiles should not be circumcised, but I say that God wants them to be circumcised. Another one may say that the Gentiles should not be required to keep the law, but I say that this is not God's leading. We have to speak what we have observed before God honestly, completely, and without reservation.

THE PATTERN IN ACTS OF FELLOWSHIPPING CONCERNING CHURCH AFFAIRS

"When much discussion had taken place"— Everyone Having Expressed Their Inner Sense

We have two patterns in Acts concerning how to fellowship about church affairs. First, we see the matter of discussion in Acts 15:7, which says, "When much discussion had taken place." In the church life there are some who seem to have no words or feelings at all. They appear to be very spiritual, but in reality they are not spiritual. When a person is learning to deal with his opinions, he often falls into a situation of being overly strict, thinking that to be silent is to be spiritual and that to speak is to be opinionated. Therefore, he completely refrains from speaking in order to be "spiritual." Actually, this is wrong. It is abnormal for a person to become so spiritual that he has no feeling. In a normal situation the leading ones in the church and the representatives of the church should gather together and should be able to discuss matters thoroughly and completely, even fellowshipping and discussing again and again. There should not be just one person speaking or just a few persons speaking, but everyone should speak and express all the feelings that they have within them. Whether they are elders or deacons, as long as they have any inner sense concerning the matter being discussed, they should speak out clearly.

"Therefore it is my opinion"—
Speaking according to One's Observation
of God's Work in the Church

Acts 15 also shows us how we should speak. In this chapter we see the patterns set up by three persons: Peter, Paul, and James. We should imitate these three persons in the way they spoke. They did not speak merely according to their own opinions but according to the observations that they had made and the sense that they had received in the church. Peter spoke according to what he had observed of God's work in the church, as did Paul and James. Do not think that they did not have any opinions. James said, "Therefore it is my opinion" (v. 19, Chinese Union Version). This shows that he had an opinion. His opinion, however, was based on the word of God. We may speak differently from one another, but we should not speak according to our own opinion. Furthermore, we should not speak according to our preference, because that kind of speaking is mostly of the flesh. If we are concerned about the church, we must learn to speak according to what we have observed. However, when we learn to speak in this way, the Chinese should not have Chinese views, and the foreigners should not have foreigners' views. That is not the practice of the church life. In the church you must fear God, and I must also fear God. You should not take the customs of the foreigners, and I should not take the ways of the Chinese. You have a part in the Lord's work, and I also have a part in the Lord's work. Thus, you should speak out what you have observed concerning the Lord's work, and I also should speak out what I have observed regarding the Lord's work.

Peter was thoroughly a Jew. However, in Acts 15 when many people were discussing, Peter spoke not according to his own opinion but according to the Lord's work. He rose up and said, "Men, brothers, you know that from the early days God chose from among you that through my mouth..." (v. 7). In today's environment hardly anyone speaks this way. On the surface we are all very humble. In the service meetings most people say, "I am not worthy to say anything. I am the least. I do not have anything to say. I do not have any opinion." Yet when the meeting is over, they express their opinions end-lessly. However, Peter was not like this. He did not speak superficially polite words. Being polite often is worse than being fleshly. Rather, Peter was speaking the truth before God without being proud. We all have to be like Peter, being completely without pride but being able to rise up to say according to the fact, "Brothers, concerning the matter of serving the Lord, I perceive that God wants us to serve in this manner." This opinion is spiritual, not subjective. It is experiential, based on the work of God, and is not fleshly.

"The Holy Spirit and...us"—
God and Man Mingled Together
Making a Decision

After Peter had finished speaking, Paul rose up to speak. Eventually, how was the matter decided? Was it according to the democratic way of the minority submitting to the majority? In Acts we see that after Peter had spoken, there was no solution, and after Paul had finished speaking, there was still no solution. One said that God gave grace to the Gentiles through him, and the other also said that God gave grace to the Gentiles through him. All those who were present in that gathering spoke thoroughly concerning what they saw related to God's work in this matter. Therefore, in Acts 15 first we see that everyone participated in the discussion. Second, we see that in the discussion they did not speak according to their own feelings but according to the result of God's work. They were delivered from their own opinions. Third, we see that the leading one among the children of God made a decision based upon the opinions expressed by everyone and also according to the principle in the holy Scriptures. Such a decision by the church and the Holy Spirit was spiritual. It was a decision not of man—neither of an individual nor of the majority—but of "the Holy Spirit and...us" (v. 28). How wonderful! It was a decision made by God mingled with man. Therefore, we do not make the decision by ourselves, but the Holy Spirit and we make the decision together.

In order to make this kind of decision, we need to learn to fear the Lord and live before Him. We need to learn to reject the flesh and the natural being. We also need to learn to be conscious of the church and of the work, just as Peter was conscious of the church and Paul was conscious of the work. This is to be spiritual. In the Scriptures the most spiritual matter is God being mingled with man. Although man is speaking, it seems that it is God who is speaking. It is the speaking of God mingled with man. It is not merely God speaking, nor is it merely man speaking. Rather, it is God speaking with man by being mingled with man, and it is man speaking under the Holy Spirit, that is, under the control and restriction of the Holy Spirit.

In addition, the elders should not decide any matter by themselves. Instead, they should observe the situation of the saints and also allow the saints to fully express in fellowship their feelings before God concerning the matter. Then the elders should make a decision not merely according to their own feelings but according to the feelings of all the children of God and according to the principles in the holy Scriptures as well.

In the church, decisions should not be made based merely on whatever the elders say. Neither should the elders make decisions by getting the consent of the majority of the saints when they are unsure of what to do. Any decision concerning church affairs must be the result of the operation of the Holy Spirit. Such a decision is neither of one individual nor of the majority but of "the Holy Spirit and...us." This is spiritual, and this is the principle for the administration of the church. The administration of the church does not depend upon the opinion of one individual or upon the opinion of the majority. Please keep in mind that all our own opinions are from the enemy. Hence, in the church service we should put all our opinions aside. This is not to say that we should not have any observations or feelings. Rather, the Holy Spirit should be moving within us, and as the saints and we are gathered together, we should all lay out our feelings before the Lord and fellowship together. Then before the Lord and according to these feelings we should make a decision under the principles shown in the holy Scriptures.

In order to have a proper administration of the church we need to put aside our flesh, opinions, narrowness, negligence, and carelessness. Some are too careless, and others are too narrow. Neither is acceptable. Some are too negligent, and others are too natural. Both of these will not do. We must let the Holy Spirit make manifest the feelings of all the saints and then make a decision based upon these feelings along with the principles revealed in the Scriptures. I am not saying that if we make decisions this way, we will never make a mistake. But I dare say that even if we make a little mistake, we will still be right according to the spiritual principle. We would rather make a mistake while doing things the right way. This is the basic principle.

A FEW POINTS OF FELLOWSHIP FOR THE ELDERS AND DEACONS WHO ARE NEW IN THE COORDINATION

Being Responsible and Accurate in Speech

Finally, I have a few points to fellowship with the elders and deacons who are new in the coordination. First, you must learn to speak accurately among the children of God. No elder can be irresponsible in his speaking, and no deacon can be inaccurate in his speaking. We truly need to be rescued in this matter. Elders and deacons need to learn to speak responsibly as well as accurately. Neither inaccurate words nor irresponsible words should be spoken. All inaccurate and irresponsible words are death. Those of you who are elders must not make a judgment based on rumors. You must remember that it is not easy to believe the truth, but it is easy to believe a lie. Today in the church there are too many irresponsible words. Every word we speak must be accurate, and we need to be accountable for our words. Otherwise, there will surely be many problems in the church.

Not Disclosing Any Matter That Has Not Yet Been Formally Decided and Announced

Before any matter that has been discussed in the service meeting is formally announced in public, neither the elders nor the deacons should go out and talk about it. This does not mean that we have any dark secrets. This is simply for the benefit of others. It is best not to talk to others about matters in the administration of the church before the matters are decided. You should not disclose these matters even to someone as close to you as your wife. Otherwise, you will offend the church. For example, suppose we have decided to have a conference but have not announced it yet. If we have made only an internal decision, we should not carelessly spread the news. Instead, we should wait until it is fully decided and formally announced before we have open fellowship about it. We should not take this matter lightly, but we must pay serious attention to this. Regardless of what you hear and see, especially concerning the matters discussed in the meetings of the elders and co-workers, you should not spread them to others. This is not because we have anything dark to hide but is for the benefit of others. Any matter related to the administration of the church should remain only in the fellowship and should not be carelessly spread outside before it is decided. If we carelessly spread information, this shows that our learning is short. If we all would understand this limitation and hold on to it, then there would be no gossiping, no scandals, and no problems in the church.

Learning to Ask More and Not Making Any Decisions on Our Own

Furthermore, all the saints in coordination must learn not to lightly make decisions on their own concerning matters about which they are not clear. The principle here is that no one should make any decision alone. Even if we are already clear, we still should ask and fellowship. Who should we ask? We should ask the elderly saints. For important matters we surely need to seek fellowship from others and find a way to solve the problem together before the Lord. The more we ask, the less likely we will be to make mistakes. In any case, it is better not to reach a decision by ourselves. In the church there are so many people and so many matters. Thus, it is not proper to make decisions on our own. Never think that it is a shame to ask others. Rather, humble yourself to be taught, and learn to ask often.

Not Having Our Own Opinion and Our Own Way

Another point is that we should not have our own opinion and our own way. We must learn to put aside our own opinions. All our opinions must be put forth in fellowship in the service meeting or in the elders' meeting. If we know that our way is not good, we should not try to get others to accommodate us. We are all people of limitation, and what we know is limited. Hence, we should learn while doing. The extent of our awareness of church affairs also shows the extent of our learning and of our being restricted before God. We need to learn to speak accurately, to not spread abroad the matters discussed in the meetings, to ask more questions, and to make less decisions on our own. Moreover, we should not hold on to our own opinions and our own ways. We need to pay attention to and learn all these things.

CHAPTER THREE

HOW TO LEAD THE NEWLY SAVED ONES

THE NEWLY SAVED ONES
NEEDING TO ADVANCE IN THREE MATTERS

A newly saved one should steadily advance in three matters. First, he must learn the lessons of life for his advancement in life. Second, he must diligently read the Bible for his advancement in the divine Word. Third, he must learn to preach the gospel for his advancement in leading people to salvation. These three matters are fundamental lessons that a Christian should learn and steadily develop. Therefore, under normal circumstances, a person who has been baptized and has entered into the church life must be perfected in these three matters.

In the church it is rather easy to arouse people and stir them up to be zealous. Encouraging people by stirring up a kind of atmosphere is not a difficult thing to do. The difficult thing is helping the newly saved ones to advance in life, to become rooted in the Word, and to labor in the service and the propagation of the gospel step by step and in a proper way. This is not an easy or ordinary task. This kind of service is special and can only be carried out by those who have been taught and trained to do so. Such ones must experience the things that they teach. Moreover, they must live in fellowship with the Lord, continually learning how to carry out this service in a proper way. Only then can they help others. First, let us look at how to lead and help the newly saved ones in the aspect of life.

ADVANCING IN LIFE

If we want to help people advance in life, first we need to help them have an accurate understanding of the matter of salvation. Although a person may have already been baptized and received into the church, he still must begin with the matter of knowing his salvation. If a person does not have a thorough understanding of his salvation, then it will be difficult for him to advance in life. Do not think that all Christians are one hundred percent assured of their salvation. Some have been saved and may even realize that they have already been saved, yet when others challenge their salvation, they may say, "I am probably not saved." They are easily shaken because they lack the knowledge of the assurance of their salvation. Hence, we need to help them establish such a firm foundation.

Helping People to Practically Establish a Foundation in Life

How do we help others have a proper understanding of salvation based upon the holy Scriptures so that they may establish a firm foundation? First we must have a basic knowledge of the Bible, and then we must lead them to the proper understanding step by step. For example, suppose we meet someone who somewhat doubts his salvation. In order to help him, we may open to Mark 16:16 and ask him to read it: "He who believes and is baptized shall be saved." After he reads it, we may ask him, "Who said this?" He would say, "The Lord Jesus said it." We then may ask him, "Are the words of the Lord Jesus false? Can they be changed?" He would say, "The words of the Lord Jesus are true and unchangeable." We must continue to ask, "How do we know that the Lord's words are unchangeable?" Then we can ask him to read Matthew 24:35, where the Lord Jesus said, "Heaven and earth will pass away, but My words shall by no means pass away." At this point we can ask him if he is clear. If he says that he is clear, then we have to ask again, "The Lord said that 'He who believes and is baptized shall be saved.' Have you believed?" He will answer, "Yes, I have believed." Then we should ask, "Have you been baptized?" He will then reply, "Yes, I have been baptized." Then we can tell him, "Since you have believed and have also been baptized, are you saved according to the Lord's word?" He might say that according to the Lord's words he is saved, but he does not feel that he is saved. Then we can ask him again, "Did the Lord say here that he who believes and is baptized and who feels it shall be saved?" He will answer, "No." Then we can ask again, "Then are you saved?" Finally, he will say, "Yes, I am saved."

Needing to Use the Scriptures in Helping People Become Clear about Their Salvation

We have to learn to be able to use the words of the Bible in helping people, especially those who have been listening to messages for years and are still not clear about their salvation. We may start with a verse such as 1 John 1:7, which says, "The blood of Jesus His Son cleanses us from every sin." We can ask the one we are helping to read it several times until he becomes familiar with it. Then we can ask him, "Who spoke this word?" He will answer, "God spoke it." Then we can ask, "Does God's word count?" He will reply, "It counts." Then we can ask further, "Then what does this word say?" He would say, "It says that the blood of Jesus His Son cleanses us from every sin." If we ask, "Whose sin does the blood of Jesus cleanse?", he would say, "It cleanses us from every sin." Then we can ask, "Does this 'us' include you?" He may think for a while and then say, "Since it says 'us,' it includes me." After this we should tell him, "Since the 'us' in this verse includes you, you should substitute it with your name and read it that way." Then he may read, "The blood of Jesus His Son cleanses me from every sin." The more he reads the verse, the more he will become familiar with it. Then we can ask him, "The blood cleanses how many of your sins?" He will then answer, "The blood of the Lord Jesus cleanses me from 'every' sin." In this way he will become clear about his salvation. Moreover, he will be clear based on his knowledge of the truth.

Helping the Newly Saved Ones to Advance in Life in Five Aspects

Helping Them to Deal with the Past

Touching Their Conscience

You may meet someone who is saved and is also fully

confident that he is saved. However, due to an insensitivity
toward sins, he has never properly confessed his sins before
God but only admits in a general way that he is sinful. How
can we help this kind of person have a thorough confession of
sins? To help remove someone's doubts concerning salvation,
we need to use the Bible, because the Bible is the only means
for man to be saved. However, to help a person become conscious of his sins, we also need to touch his conscience. The
doctrine concerning man's sinfulness is easy to understand.
After hearing it, a person can immediately understand it in
his mind. Hence, he does not need a great deal of teaching.
What he needs is for someone to knock on his conscience and
touch his conscience so that it will become sensitive. This is
the principle the Lord Jesus applied in John 4 while He was
speaking with the Samaritan woman by the well.

On that day by the well in Sychar the Lord Jesus did
not tell the Samaritan woman, "You were sinful from your
mother's womb." John chapter four does not directly mention
the matter of sin. It does not even mention the word *sin*.
When the Samaritan woman asked the Lord for the living
water, the Lord told her to go call her husband. She became
afraid when asked about her husband, because her sins were
all related to her husbands. Which one could she ask to come?
One was divorced from her, another was finished with her,
and the current one was questionable. So in answering the
Lord she told a lie by speaking the truth, saying, "I do not
have a husband." The Lord Jesus then said, "You have well
said, I do not have a husband, for you have had five husbands,
and the one you now have is not your husband" (vv. 17-18).
After the Lord told her this, her conscience was awakened.
Then she said to the Lord, "I perceive that You are a prophet"
(v. 19). It is not necessary to say so much about sin. As long as
we can touch someone in his conscience, his conscience will
give him a sense of pain, and this sense of pain will lead him
to kneel before the Lord to confess his sins. We all have had
this kind of experience. We may start by confessing one sin,
but then we confess a second sin and a third. No one can
claim in a loose way that he has no sin, for we all have sinned.

We have to lead a new believer to deal with the past step

by step. If he has offended others, he has to ask for their forgiveness. If he owes others something, he has to make restitution. If he has cheated others, he has to confess to them. He has to deal with the past to such an extent that he can stand before God and men with a conscience void of offense.

Helping Them to Know that Dealing with the Conscience Is for Them to Walk the Path before Them

In order to advance, a Christian must have a conscience without leaks. If a Christian's conscience has leaks, it is like a car with a leaky engine. A Christian's conscience must not have any leaks. Many people who have been saved may have a conscience that has never been whole but has always had leaks. Someone like this may have cheated someone else of a dollar before he was saved. Now as a saved one he has twenty dollars, yet he is still unwilling to return the dollar he stole. His sin has already been forgiven, yet the fact of sin, the scar of sin, is still there. The reason for this is not that there is no accusation within him but that his conscience is deflated. Therefore, when we lead others in dealing with the past, we must help them understand that this is not for them to "go to heaven" but for them to properly walk the path before them.

Helping Them to Consecrate Themselves to God

We also have to help the newly saved ones to consecrate themselves to God and to know that the meaning of consecration is not mainly to work for God but to be gained by God. God intends to do a great deal of work in us, but He requires our consent. We give Him our consent by consecrating ourselves to Him so that He may work freely in us. If we want to bring people before God in this way, it is not sufficient to merely have the doctrine. We must have the real experience and the real way.

Helping Them to Obey the Sense of Life

We have to lead people to know that the Lord dwells in us as the Spirit and as life, causing us to have an inner sense concerning many matters. We must obey this sense, and we must also see that being a Christian is not an outward matter but an inward matter. As Christians, we behave ourselves not according to the outward letter but according to the living Person—the living God—within us. This living God within us gives us a sense. Therefore, we should live according to this inner sense.

Helping Them to Have Fellowship with the Lord

At the same time we also need to help people learn to have fellowship with the Lord. The Lord in whom we believe and whom we serve is living. Furthermore, He lives in us and is with us in every place and at every time. Hence, we must always be in union with Him, approach Him, and enjoy Him.

Helping Them to Have a Prayer Life

In addition to the above four points, we also have to help the newly saved ones know through prayer that the One in whom they believe is the true and living God, and we must also help them experience Him in prayer.

In summary, we need to help and lead the newly saved ones in these five points: first, dealing with the past; second, consecration; third, obeying the sense of life; fourth, having fellowship with the Lord; and fifth, having a prayer life before God and learning to know God in prayer. When they learn these five points they can be considered to be advancing in life.

Practically Knowing Christ as Our Life

In addition to the above five points, we have to go a step further to practically help them to know that the Christ who is within them is their life and their light of life. Furthermore, we have to help them to know that although they were previously in Adam, they are now in Christ and have been united with Christ to be one with Him. Upon seeing this union, they will then realize that Christ is their life.

Today there are thousands and thousands of saved ones, but not many have experientially seen the fact of their position in Christ or of their union with Christ. Many people zealously love the Lord and preach the gospel. They also pray frequently, deal with their sins, and often obey the sense of life. However, very few truly know what their salvation means—that in Christ they have been united with Christ and that Christ today is in them to be their life and power, enabling them to be delivered from themselves, to deny themselves, to reject themselves, and thereby to live Christ. We need to know the Christ who is within us, to know that once we were in Adam but now we have been transferred into Christ and have Christ as our life. Therefore, we can reject ourselves and live in Christ.

The first step in leading people in the Christian experience is to lead them to salvation. Then we must help them to have the assurance of salvation, to deal with the past, to consecrate themselves, to obey the sense within, to have fellowship with God, and to pray. These are the initial experiences of a Christian. The second step is to help people see that they were originally in Adam but now have been transferred into Christ and that Christ is dwelling in them to be their life. With such a realization, a person will then be able to reject his self and live in Christ. Salvation is a Christian's experience in the first stage whereas rejecting the self and living in Christ is his experience in the second stage.

From the book of Romans we see that the Christian experience begins when a sinner is saved and consummates when he is mature in life. The first stage of the Christian experience is salvation, and the second stage is being in Christ. In the church life today most of the believers are lingering in the first experience and have not yet entered into the second experience. They remain only in their consecration, their zeal, their limited fellowship with the Lord, and their limited prayer. We need to lead the brothers and sisters into the second experience of a Christian—being in Christ and realizing that to be in Christ is to experience His death and resurrection.

BEING ROOTED IN THE READING OF THE WORD

Next, we need to help the newly saved ones to be rooted in the reading of the Word. We need to lead the brothers and sisters to study the holy Scriptures properly. In particular, there are brothers and sisters among us who are students. For these ones we need to have a systematic, section by section reading of the Word of God, studying it as if we were studying a science. Many people have done extensive research regarding education and have made great achievements in scientific research, but their study of the Holy Bible is very poor. When they talk about the Bible, they are just like children drawing pictures that are missing this part and that part. To them it seems that Matthew and Mark are almost the same, Mark and Luke are almost the same, and Luke and John are also almost the same. Everything is muddled. You must realize that without a systematic study of the Holy Bible, no Christian can have a clear, fundamental understanding of the truth or make progress in the truth.

Only when a Christian has a clear understanding of the Word can he have real advancement in life. The young people in particular must realize that after the age of fifty, a person cannot learn so well. Those who have studied know that after a person passes the age of thirty, it is somewhat difficult to go back to school. Therefore, we have to properly lead people to read the holy Scriptures after they are saved. However, even many of us who have been saved for many years may not have spent enough effort on the Bible in a good way. This causes us grief and greatly concerns us. We must make a strong determination to spend more effort to study the Bible. Then we will be able to lead and help the newly saved ones to read the Bible also. We have to read Romans at least a hundred times, Ephesians at least a hundred and fifty times, and 1 Corinthians seventy times. We have to make a real effort to read the Lord's word. This is the truth, the way, and the life.

The outpouring of the Holy Spirit has to be matched with the knowledge of the truth and of life. In order to grow real things in the church, we need to sow real seeds. If real seeds are sown, then the growth in the church will continue, even if the weather is dry. The real seeds are the truth and life. However, without the support of the holy Scriptures, the truth is empty, and without the support of the Holy Spirit, the truth is not practical. For this reason, God gave us the Holy Bible without and the Holy Spirit within. Therefore, we must properly know the Word and study it seriously. The clearer we are in our reading the better.

LEARNING IN THE GOSPEL

Besides helping the newly saved ones in their advancement in life and in their being rooted in the reading of the Word, we need to help them in the matter of gospel preaching. Immediately after someone is saved, we have to lead him to begin preaching the gospel. If possible, we need to bring him into the service in the church, perhaps even beginning with mopping the floor. I hope that none of us would take this matter lightly. If we lead the newly saved ones to advance in these three matters, then the church in our locality will be firmly established.

CHAPTER FOUR

HOW TO RECEIVE THE SAVED ONES

For about two thousand years there have been various disputes in the church concerning the qualifications for believing in the Lord and being saved. The proper way to resolve this matter is to come back to the Bible. We must remember, however, that the New Testament service is a service of the Spirit and not of the letter. Therefore, when we read the New Testament, we should not search for a set of rules on how to handle a certain matter. If the Bible gave us a set of rules to follow, then we would not need to serve according to the Spirit. To do things according to regulations is not the service of the Spirit. Hence, there are no clearly defined rules concerning the receiving of those who are saved in the New Testament. It only mentions one point here and another point there and gives us one pattern here and another pattern there. In this way it allows us to learn how to touch the spiritual reality.

Although we do not have to keep a set of ordinances according to the letter in order to touch the spiritual reality, this does not mean that there are no principles or light in the Scriptures. In the Bible God uses plain words and patterns to show us the kind of person who may be baptized, who may be recognized as our brother or sister, and who has received the Lord's grace and may be received into the church.

THE EARLY CHURCH RECEIVING THE BELIEVERS ACCORDING TO THE HOLY SCRIPTURES

According to church history, before the Catholic Church came into being, the church received people, baptized them, and called them brothers and sisters according to the holy

Scriptures. Their outward situation forced them to do these
things according to the Scriptures, because at that time the
Roman emperors were greatly persecuting the church, persecuting anyone who believed in the Lord and confessed that he
was a Christian. Under such an atmosphere of persecution
the church had no problem regarding receiving the believers.

DIFFERENT WAYS OF BAPTIZING PEOPLE
IN TRADITIONAL CHRISTIANITY

Early in the fourth century the Roman general Constantine, desiring to gain the Roman Empire, vowed that if he
gained control of the Roman Empire, he would embrace
Christianity as the religion of the empire. Later, after gaining
control of the empire, he issued an order asking all the
citizens to join the Christian religion and rewarding with
silver and garments all those who joined. Thus, almost all the
citizens of the Roman Empire joined Christianity. During this
time the church became deformed. The Bible tells us that
the church is like a mustard seed (Matt. 13:31), which is a
small seed of life that produces a small herb. However, when
Constantine accepted the Christian religion and made it the
imperial religion, the church was completely changed in its
character and became deformed. Originally it had been a
small herb, but it became a great perennial tree—the Catholic
Church. Not only is this great tree deformed, the birds of
heaven—Satan and his evil spirits—also come and roost in it.
The mutated Roman imperial church baptized people regardless of whether they had repented and confessed their sins or
whether they had the life of God. As long as a person was a
Roman citizen, he could be baptized.

After the Roman Catholic Church was officially formed,
the membership began to include not only Roman citizens but
also people of other nations. The only requirement for them
to be baptized was that they had to acknowledge the God of
the Catholic Church. As long as a person acknowledged the
God of the Catholic Church, he could be baptized. Later, the
Episcopalian church was formed. To be baptized by the Episcopalian church of a certain country, a person had to meet
only one qualification—he had to be a citizen of that country.

For instance, the Anglican Church did not ask if a person was saved or not. As long as he was British, he could be baptized. If a person did not wish to join the state church, he could join any of the private churches, which were more advanced than the state churches. For example, the Methodist church founded by John Wesley told people that anyone who wanted to escape the future wrath could be baptized. They said this based on Matthew 3:7b, which says, "Who prompted you to flee from the coming wrath?" In the preaching of the gospel, John Wesley was quite proper, but in baptizing and receiving people, his requirement was too arbitrary.

Among the private churches, the Presbyterians and the Lutherans have similar practices. They ask people to learn their doctrines and then baptize them only when they understand the doctrines. They ask the candidates to listen to the preaching of the word and to pursue the word. Then after the candidates pass an examination, they are baptized. There are also some denominations that baptize babies. As long as someone is a member of that denomination, his children can be baptized soon after birth. All these practices are unscriptural.

RECEIVING PEOPLE ACCORDING TO THE BIBLE

Believing and Being Baptized

When we receive people by baptizing them, we must do it not according to the practices in traditional Christianity but according to the Bible. First of all let us see what kind of person can be baptized. The Bible says, "He who believes and is baptized shall be saved" (Mark 16:16). What then is the basis for baptism? Obviously, baptism is based upon believing. There are many such cases in Acts. Chapter eight, for example, tells us about Philip baptizing the Ethiopian eunuch. As Philip and the eunuch were going along the road, they came upon water, and the eunuch said, "Look, water. What prevents me from being baptized?" (v. 36). Philip answered, "If you believe from all your heart, you will be saved" (v. 37). Besides this, there was no other requirement. In chapters eighteen and nineteen there are also examples of many who believed and were baptized.

On the day of Pentecost Peter told the people, "Repent and each one of you be baptized upon the name of Jesus Christ for the forgiveness of your sins" (2:38). The phrase *upon the name of Jesus Christ* indicates that the people had believed in the Lord Jesus, because without believing they could not have been baptized upon the name of Jesus Christ. Therefore, the unique basis for baptism is our faith.

Faith Being Not an Acknowledging in the Mind but a Receiving in the Spirit

However, faith is not so simple. First, we must know what faith is, and then we must know how to discern whether or not a person has this faith. Faith is not a mental understanding or acknowledgement. Mental understanding, consent, or acknowledgment is not faith. Faith is not a matter of the mind. Faith is a receiving in the spirit. The faith spoken of in the Bible, particularly in the New Testament, refers to our relationship with the Lord—our union with Him—through faith. For example, John 3:15 says, "That every one who believes into Him may have eternal life." The preposition used here is *into,* not *upon* or *besides,* indicating that we enter into the Lord by believing.

Romans 6:3 says, "Or are you ignorant that all of us who have been baptized into Christ Jesus have been baptized into His death?" In Chinese *into* seems to be a verb, but actually it is a preposition. We may use the turning on of a switch as an illustration. When we turn on the switch of a lamp, electricity flows into the lamp, joining the lamp to the power plant. The lamp has been installed in our house, but the electricity for the lamp is in the power plant. When we believe in the Lord Jesus, the Lord Jesus immediately enters into us as the Spirit and as life. As a result, we have a life relationship, an organic union, with Christ. To believe into Christ is not to understand something in the mind, to mentally agree with or acknowledge a doctrine. Rather, it is the spirit within man touching Christ. When a person contacts Christ in his spirit, by faith he enters into Christ. This is the faith referred to in the Bible. This faith is the basis for our baptizing people.

Repenting before Believing and Calling after Believing

A person has to repent before he believes. No one can believe without repenting. After repenting, a person naturally sees that the Lord Jesus is the Savior and that the Lord died for him on the cross. When he receives the Lord in this way, that is, when he believes, the Holy Spirit and the life of Christ enter into him. Thus, this person is born again. Therefore, before believing, there is repentance. Of course, after believing there surely will be calling. Everyone who repents and believes uses his mouth to call on the Lord. Acts 2:21 says, "Everyone who calls on the name of the Lord shall be saved." However, those who merely use their minds to understand and acknowledge do not call.

When I first believed in the Lord, people asked me if I was sinful, and I said that I was. When people said that there was God, I agreed that there was God. This God, however, had no effect or impact within me because I understood Him and agreed with Him only in my mind. Therefore, when I was baptized, although I agreed with the doctrine of man's sinfulness, I had no consciousness of sin within me. I had never grieved or felt sorry for my sins. Although I acknowledged the death of the Lord Jesus on the cross, I was not moved by that death; I only acknowledged it mentally. A year later, after being enlightened through the work of the Holy Spirit within me, I not only admitted that I was sinful, but I also felt that I was sinful. Being exceedingly sorrowful in my heart, I did not cease repenting for my sins and confessing them. I remember that the day I was enlightened, I prayed on a mountain while beating myself and confessing my sins. I went to God, no longer understanding a doctrine just in my mind but truly being conscious of my wrongdoings. That was my real believing into the Lord. This kind of believing gives us an inner sense and causes us to call on the Lord. Therefore, before believing, there must be repentance, and after believing, there must be calling.

Whenever we baptize and receive someone, instead of asking him how much he understands, we should ask him whether or not he has believed. If a person has not touched the Lord in his spirit, then even if he has memorized the entire Bible, he is still unsaved. The chief priests and scribes were thoroughly familiar with the Scriptures. Therefore, when King Herod inquired of them where the Christ was to be born, immediately they replied, "In Bethlehem of Judea" (Matt. 2:4-5). To know the Bible in the mind is one matter, but to contact Christ in the spirit is another matter. The magi who sought the Lord did not understand even one verse of the Scriptures, yet they were able to find the child Jesus and to offer gifts to Him (v. 11). Therefore, when we intend to baptize someone, we should not focus on examining him to find out how much doctrine he understands. Rather, we must touch him to determine whether or not he has believed.

The Experience of Salvation and Regeneration

There is a story of a person who had been a preacher for many years. One day after a meeting he was standing by the entrance of the chapel. The missionary who had delivered the sermon that day approached him and asked, "Have you been born again?" This missionary preached specifically on repentance and regeneration, and whenever he met people, he would ask if they were born again. This preacher then replied, "I have been born again." The missionary nodded his head and said, "The way you look shows that you have not yet been born again. You say that you have been born again, but your tone reveals that you have not been born again." When the preacher went home, the more he thought about the matter, the angrier he became. He felt that he had been humiliated in public, and he considered going to the missionary and beating him up. At this juncture, God's sovereignty was manifested, and the Holy Spirit worked within him, saying, "How could you be such a bad person? Someone told you that you have not been regenerated, and you want to beat him up?" He considered it a little bit and then felt that it really was true that he had not been regenerated. Then he knelt down and confessed his sins, realizing that although he was no longer a bad person, had joined the church, and had become a preacher, inwardly he was still wicked to the uttermost. The more he confessed, the more sorrowful he became. After praying, however, he became so joyful within that he could not wait until the next meeting. He immediately went to the missionary's home. When the missionary opened the door and saw the preacher, he said, "Congratulations, you have been saved and born again!"

ILLUSTRATIONS OF RECEIVING PEOPLE ACCORDING TO THE HOLY SCRIPTURES

All of us who have had the experience of salvation and have been brought through it by God know what it is to be saved, to repent and turn to God, to contact the Lord, and to have the presence of the Lord. We also know what inward repentance and the sense of the spirit are. In regard to contacting people, there may be a number of ways to sense a person's condition within, but the reality of his condition is the same. Because we often do not see people's inward condition, we may receive someone who has the doctrinal understanding but does not have the Lord in him, or we may reject someone who has the Lord within but is confused concerning doctrine. When the church in Foochow started to have a revival, there were many young people who were saved and wanted to be baptized. This forced us to put aside all our old, traditional practices. One time during an interview for a baptism, I asked the student who wanted to be baptized, "Would you feel good about giving the coat you are wearing now to the poor?" He said, "Yes." I asked him why, and he said, "Since the Lord Jesus shed His blood on the cross for me, how could I not give this coat to others?" At this point there was no need to ask him how many gods there are or who the Triune God is. If you ask people with your mind, they will answer you with their mind, but if you ask them questions that touch their inner being, their condition within will be clearly revealed.

I asked another one, "Why are you here?" He said, "I am here to be baptized." I asked, "Why do you want to be baptized?" He said, "I am saved." I asked, "How do you know that you are saved?" He said, "I used to enjoy watching movies.

Even when my mother prohibited me, I still watched them. However, ever since I heard the gospel and received the Lord Jesus, I have seen how lovely the Lord is, so I do not watch movies anymore." At that point there was no need to ask him, "Do you believe in the eternal life? Do you believe in the coming judgment?" He surely believed. I asked still another one, "What is the meaning of baptism?" He said, "Baptism means that we have died with the Lord and were buried with Him and that we are no longer in union with the world. Although I am not clear yet about the Bible, once I am baptized, I want nothing else besides the Lord." You can baptize this kind of person without asking him anything further.

This may be likened to buying flour. When we go to the flour mill to buy flour, we do not need to open the sacks one by one to look at the contents. We only need to stick a testing needle into the sack and then draw it out and look. In this way we know what is inside. Do not test people's minds. Instead, try to touch their inner condition. Some say that this way of interviewing for baptism is too quick and may not be dependable. However, wheat flour is always wheat flour. You cannot turn it into rice by opening the sack and studying it. We care about the real condition within a person. Has he really met God? Has he received the Lord as his Savior? Has he repented? Has he called on the Lord? Does he sense God's presence? We want to touch the real situation within a man to see if he is truly saved. Doctrines received in the mind have no effect on a person's salvation. Some people do not understand the doctrine, but they have a living Lord within them who is their life and is reigning within them. This is the way to receive people based upon the Scriptures.

CHAPTER FIVE

TWO MATTERS CONCERNING SERVICE

The service of the Body in the church is a matter of coordination and a matter of authority.

THE COORDINATION OF THE BODY

A Christian has several statuses before God. In receiving grace in God's house, every saved one is a child of God. In loving the Lord Jesus, every saved one is like a virgin presented to Him. Concerning service, however, every saved one is member of the Body of Christ. Therefore, the matter of Christian service and the matter of coordination in the Body always go together, because it is impossible for a member to exist and live by himself. Once a member is alone and by himself, he immediately loses his existence and function. Christian service is a corporate service, not an individual service. Hence, we must be freed from our independence.

In service, we not only need to be freed from sins and the self; we also need to be freed even more from our independence. Our problem is that we have our own views and opinions and therefore have no way to coordinate with others. On the surface, our service may appear to be corporate and not individual, but in reality there may be very little that is truly corporate in our service. Apparently our service may be corporate, but in actuality it may be the service of a few individuals. The reason for this is the lack of the reality of coordination.

Service is especially manifested in the Body of Christ. Once service to God in the church is mentioned in the Bible, it is immediately linked to the members of the Body. Every saved one is a member. While you are serving God together with the brothers and sisters, do you feel that there is a relationship between you and the other members? When you coordinate with a brother in the church, do you feel like you are the hand and he is the arm? Do you feel that it is impossible for you and him to be freed from one another, that there is no way for you to become detached, independent, or separated? We must admit that we seldom have this kind of feeling.

Having the Consciousness of the Body in Our Service in Coordination

In our service to God, we must be brought by God to the point where we have the consciousness of the Body and do not serve individually but in coordination with the brothers and sisters. We must be brought to a point where the brothers' move is our move, and our move is the brothers' move. Regardless of the circumstance we are in, our feeling should always be that what the brothers are doing is no different from what we are doing. The two should be the same.

Not only so, whenever there is a problem in our coordination with the Body, we should sense it immediately. When our coordination with all the members is normal, we may not have much feeling that we are in coordination. This is similar to the coordination in our body. In a normal situation the members of our body do not have much feeling about each other's existence. However, when a certain member has a problem, then there is a consciousness. Therefore, if we sense the existence of a certain member, then that member must have a problem. When we are particularly conscious of our eyes, something must be wrong with our eyes.

For instance, when we begin to learn how to serve, we may constantly feel that we are unclean. We may pray, "O Lord, cleanse me. Forgive me of all my offenses." Later, going a step further, we may feel that we are peculiar, that we do not have any strength, and that we have not accomplished anything in our service. A person who serves the Lord should have feelings of this kind. It is abnormal to not have feelings. If we can quarrel with our spouse at home yet serve God without any feeling, this indicates that there is a big problem in our spiritual condition.

Two Kinds of Isolation in Service

In serving, one may have the deep experience of feeling isolated. There are two reasons why one may have this sense. One reason is that as we are advancing spiritually, others may be unable to keep pace with us. Thus, we become isolated even though this is not our desire. A negative reason is that there is some factor in us that makes us unable to coordinate with others or that makes others unable to coordinate with us. Hence, we become isolated. If we feel isolated not because we desire to be isolated but because others are not able to keep pace with us, then there is nothing wrong with our feeling isolated. However, if we are isolated because we have a problem with coordination, then there is something wrong. Although this feeling is not a good feeling, it is nonetheless deep and real. This feeling that causes us to be aware of our problems is a feeling that a serving one should experience.

Life Issuing in Spontaneous Coordination

We must realize that there are two kinds of coordination. One kind is the coordination involved in outward arrangements such as sweeping the floor, cleaning the chairs, and dusting the windows. This kind of coordination is not very deep. The other kind of coordination is a coordination that grows out of the life within and is spiritual. This coordination is deeper and more real. This kind of coordination requires that our natural being, the world, our disposition, and our flesh all be dealt with so that the Lord can grow out of us. When He grows out of you and me, we are spontaneously in coordination.

Coordination Making Our Self Manifest

While learning to serve the Lord, many have had the experience that as soon as they were put in the coordination their condition was exposed. When they were at home praying, reading the Word, or pursuing the Lord, they did not sense their own condition very much. When they went out by themselves to preach the gospel and distribute gospel tracts, they also were not very conscious of their condition. However, once they began to serve together with the saints, their self immediately became manifest, particularly in their opinions, because opinions are the best representative of a person's self.

Many schools hold three-legged races during field day. In this race, the legs of two schoolmates are tied together, one student's right leg being tied to the other student's left leg. Thus, two persons with four legs become two persons with three legs. If the two do not coordinate properly in the race, for example, if one walks quickly while the other walks slowly, then they will not only be unable to walk but might even fall down. Then they may begin to blame each other. Similarly, until two persons are put together in coordination, they will not realize how strong they are in their disposition. Once we are put in coordination with the saints, we discover how much of the self we have and how strong we are in our disposition.

Coordination Being Mainly
Not for Right or Wrong but for Dealing
with Our Self and Individualism

Suppose five of us are serving in coordination to dust the chairs, and suddenly I suggest that we turn the chairs over with the legs pointing upward. How would you react? This would be a test to you. Immediately opinions and thoughts would rise up from within you. You must realize that the most important thing in the church service is not that we perform our tasks successfully. Rather, the important matter in our serving together in coordination is how much our flesh, our disposition, and our individualism are being dealt with. When we who serve the Lord are coordinating together, the main thing is that our flesh and our disposition are dealt with. The emphasis of our service in coordination is not on whether a certain matter is right or wrong nor on whether the reason behind a matter is right or wrong. Rather, the emphasis is on whether or not our person is right and on whether or not the life is right.

In the service of the church, to be able to bear responsibility together for a year or so without any opinions is a rare and commendable thing. Usually, in order to keep opinions out of the service, everybody tries to be polite to one another. However, when we become truly serious in bearing a certain responsibility, our opinions quickly come out. The reason is that our flesh and disposition have not been broken, and the Lord has not yet touched our individualism.

There is a common Chinese saying: "Politeness maintains peace, but seriousness creates hostility." In the church service, if we can refrain from being angry when the brothers get serious with us, this indicates that our flesh has been dealt with to a great extent. In the book of Galatians, when Paul saw that what Peter did was inconsistent with the truth of the gospel, he rebuked him to his face (2:14). Both of them were very serious, but neither of them turned hostile toward the other. The biggest reason the church service is not strong and does not have much blessing is that the reality of coordination is missing. Our coordination in service has to be so real that it surpasses human organization and is as organic as the human body.

SUBMISSION TO AUTHORITY

Knowing Authority

We all know that in the service of the Body the first thing is coordination, and the second thing is authority. Some people think that authority pertains to only a few, such as apostles or elders—special kinds of people with authority. However, this is not the authority we refer to. We are referring to the authority in the Body. On the one hand, the head is the only authority of all the members of our physical body. Besides the head, no other member can exercise authority over the other members. On the other hand, every member has a member to which it submits, and at the same time every member also exercises authority over some other members. A hand has to submit to the authority of the arm, and at the same time this hand is also the authority over many fingers. Therefore, the fingers are under the authority of the hand, the hand is under the authority of the arm, and the arm is under the authority of the shoulder. However, the shoulder can only be the authority to the arms, the hands, and the fingers. It has no way to be the authority to the legs. It is the same way in the service in the Body of Christ.

Knowing Our Position

If we have been dealt with properly before the Lord and have properly learned our position, we will know who is before us as our authority and who is behind us—the ones to whom we are the authority. In a family with five siblings, does the family have to vote for someone to be the eldest brother, the second, and so on? There is no need to vote to see who is to be the oldest brother or who is to be the second. When we are placed among the brothers and sisters, immediately we know our seniority and position among them.

The life of the Lord is not an individualistic life but the Body life. In God's ordination we are all members. Since we are members, we cannot escape being in coordination with others. Since we are in the coordination, how can there not be someone over us as our authority? Suppose an arm says, "The body imprisons me. I would like to escape so that I will not have to submit to its authority." If this arm escapes, it will surely die. You may feel comfortable if I shook your hand. However, if I cut off my hand and placed it on you, would you feel so comfortable? When a member is severed from the body, it becomes something dreadful and becomes altogether useless.

The Proper Service in Coordination— Having No Self and Not Being Independent

As Christians in the Body we should know who is our authority. When we are serving in the church, there are some brothers and sisters whom we may not have to take heed to, but there are others whom we cannot disregard. The hand may contend with the ear and the nose. As a matter of fact, it may argue with almost any member and still be all right, but there is one member with whom it may not dispute—the arm. Once it has a conflict or a dispute with the arm, it is finished. Who is our authority? Others cannot decide for us. We know it in our heart. Once we know who our authority is, we have no choice but to submit. Perhaps two brothers who are neither elders nor deacons are our authority. We still have to submit to them. This is the authority in the coordination of the church service. The greatest problem in the church is our independence. The requirement in the church service is coordination. Therefore, in the church service we should not be in the self, nor should we be independent. Only then can we have normal service in coordination.

CHAPTER SIX

A FEW QUESTIONS CONCERNING REVELATION AND RELIGION

SERVING ACCORDING TO REVELATION

Suppose a person already has the concept of serving God before he is saved. Then after he believes in the Lord and is saved, he begins to serve. Is such a service according to religion or according to revelation?

To determine whether someone's service is according to revelation or religion, we need to determine whether or not his service comes from the teaching and revelation of the holy Scriptures. Sometimes a person's service originates from both his religious concept and the revelation in the Bible. We all were born in religion. We were born with religious concepts, and these concepts have been deeply rooted in us. However, the revelation of the Scriptures is working in us to get rid of our religious concepts. Nothing hinders the true revelation more than religious concepts.

In Christ

Day after day the life of Christ is growing in us. When that life is lived out of us, love is expressed. This love is much higher than man's love. Man's love in its best condition is like copper; it cannot be like gold. However, the love that issues from our living in Christ is a "golden" love—the unchangeable, eternal, divine love. The love that issues from our living in religion is not the real love, the "golden" love. Instead, it is like copper or, even worse, dirt. However, the love that issues from our living in Christ is the real love, the love that is of gold.

According to Revelation

To love people according to religious concepts is pretense. It is the love of a politician. Sometimes people polish copper until it is shiny and looks like gold. Then they offer it to us, saying that it looks like gold and is just as good. However, we should ask ourselves whether we want copper or gold. If we want gold, then we must not be fooled into accepting copper. How can we avoid being fooled? Remember that whatever is according to religion and not according to revelation is false and deceptive. Even our meeting together is not exempt from the possibility of being according to religion. We should not gather together because of human factors. If we meet together because of a few responsible ones or because of a preacher, we are accursed. We are taking this way today because we have seen that this is the Lord's way and the Lord's intention. Even if all the leading ones were to leave to pursue the world, even if they all fell in this way, we would still stand on this ground. Whether we stand on this ground or not does not depend on anyone else. Rather, it depends directly on God.

Not according to
Human Affection or Outward Things

When the Lord's recovery was first raised up, we were exercised to be absolute. We did not give favors to people in order to gain their acceptance. We did not show people humility in order to gain them. Instead, those who saw that this was the Lord's way came this way, and those who did not see that this was the Lord's way did not come. We did not use favors or humility to lead, draw, and gather people. Because of this some people said that we were proud. However, we would rather be proud than have people take this way because of our outward humility. We would rather be indifferent toward people than have people take this way merely because we love them.

Out of Christ

Any light we received through natural methods and not by reading the Scriptures is of religion. It does not matter whether we received it early in life or later. It is of religion, and the Bible refers to it as wood, grass, and stubble (1 Cor. 3:12b). Do not think that wood, grass, and stubble denote sins. Actually, they denote our work for the Lord, which may appear to be a service to Him but may not actually be out of Him. First Corinthians 3 tells us, "For another foundation no one is able to lay besides that which is laid, which is Jesus Christ" (v. 11). The foundation is Christ, and what is being built upon it is also Christ—gold, silver, and precious stones (v. 12a). Everything that is out of Christ is gold, silver, and precious stones. Everything that is out of man is wood, grass, and stubble.

THE RELATIONSHIP BETWEEN RELIGION AND REVELATION

While preaching the gospel, if we speak about escaping the vanity of life, yet we ourselves have not had the experience of escaping the vanity of life, is this not also being religious?

Our Knowledge of Christ Starting with Religion

Remember that religion is still useful. What good is a chicken if it has only feathers but no flesh? What good is a clove of garlic if it has only the outer skin and no substance inside? If one has the Christian religion but does not have Christ, then he is finished. Chicken feathers can be found everywhere, but chicken meat is not as readily available. Garlic skins can be found in garbage cans everywhere, but the garlic itself has been eaten already. In the same way, if someone wants to receive God's salvation, he must be in Christ. However, the amazing thing is that man still has to start with religion in order to know Christ.

In John 3 Nicodemus came to the Lord Jesus in the night and said, "Rabbi, we know that You have come from God as a teacher" (v. 2). Yet the Lord Jesus said to him, "Unless one is born anew, he cannot see the kingdom of God" (v. 3). Nicodemus said in surprise, "How can a man be born when he is old?" (v. 4). The Lord Jesus said, "So must the Son of Man be lifted up" (v. 14). It is no wonder that on the day the Lord

Jesus was crucified, Nicodemus came to the Lord while all the disciples fled. The cross was a stumbling block to Peter and John, yet it was a salvation to Nicodemus. Eventually, Christ entered into Nicodemus. Nevertheless, do not forget that Nicodemus's coming to the Lord started with religion.

Religion Being Only a Process, a Staircase

The case of the Samaritan woman is similar. In effect, she said to the Lord Jesus, "You, the Jews, say that men must worship God in Jerusalem, but we, the Samaritans, worship God in this mountain." The Lord Jesus answered that men should worship God neither in Jerusalem nor in any mountain but in spirit (4:20-24). Therefore, many times when we preach the gospel, we can get through only by using religion. The ones we preach to need to pass through religion and Christianity. These things are only a process. After they have gained Christ, they must break away from religion and even from Christianity. Religion, including Christianity, is only a process, a staircase.

We have had religious concepts from our birth. However, one day God brought us out of the world. We began to have a taste for God and entered into Christianity, and afterward we felt quite good and quite different. Then eventually we entered into Christ. Today many people have never touched Christ. Instead, they remain in Christianity. We have to come out of everything that is of Christianity and enter into the reality of Christ. In this process, what concerns us the most is that people who cannot touch the high thing—Christ—often ruin the lower things—religion. Please remember, even the lowest things have their usefulness. For instance, in our preaching of the gospel sometimes we have to tell people that they need peace and joy. Peace and joy are religious concepts, but in preaching the gospel we sometimes still need them.

People obtain peace and joy through the Lord Jesus. Gradually, however, we need to lead them to be freed from these things. We need to tell them that believing in Jesus is not for obtaining peace and joy or for going to heaven but simply for gaining Christ. Perhaps they may be puzzled, thinking that in saying this we mean that they should come to the meetings. After we lead them to salvation, we need to let them know that with the children of God all things will pass away except for Christ, who is everything and who will never pass away.

CHAPTER SEVEN

THE ALTAR OF GOD

THE BARRIER BETWEEN MAN AND GOD

After man fell, there was not only a barrier between him and God but also a distance. Originally man lived before God in the garden of Eden and had a face to face relationship with God. There was no barrier or distance between man and God. After man fell, however, many things entered into man that became a barrier between him and God.

If we want to live out Christ in our Christian living, we need to have fellowship with the Lord. Only the Lord's life in us can enable us to spontaneously live Him out. However, sometimes it seems very difficult to have fellowship with the Lord because there are many persons, things, and matters that alienate us from the Lord, preventing us from having fellowship with Him. God placed the tree of life and also the tree of the knowledge of good and evil in the garden of Eden. In the New Testament, when the Lord appeared to the disciples after His resurrection, He said to Peter, "Do you love Me more than these?" (John 21:15). The Lord was comparing the things in front of Peter—the fish, the net, and the sea—with Himself. In the same manner, the Lord often places something between us and Him to see if we love Him more than that thing. Only a comparison can manifest how deep our love toward Him is. Therefore, the Lord's way is to place persons, things, or matters before us in order to see whether or not we love Him more than them.

Man cannot live life in an indifferent way, because within man there is a desire to love. God created man in this way so that man would love Him. Man cannot live apathetically; he is always looking for something to love. Thus, God Himself came to be the object of man's love. Apart from God, whatever man loves will ultimately be harmful to him, no matter how good it is. No matter what man loves, he can only love it to a certain extent, because the thing he loves may be harmful to him. Therefore, if man loves something apart from the Lord without limitation, eventually he will be hurt. Only loving God, approaching God, and taking God as our joy is not harmful to us. On the contrary, loving God is better than loving anything else. We should allow God to regulate us not only in certain matters but in all matters.

We all know that we should love God, but sometimes it seems that we are not able to love Him. This is because our behavior is mostly formed by our habits. If we were to frequently study a certain thing or matter and get to know it intimately, after a while it would become part of our habit. Then we would have an affection for it, which would eventually produce love. In the same way, the more we draw near to God, love God, and consider God, the more we will spontaneously have a sense of affection toward God. Ultimately we will not be able to stop loving God. In this way God will be able to enter into us and into all our situations in order to regulate us in every way.

In practice, for us to live such a life of drawing near to God and loving God, we must do four things every day. First, we need to speak to God. This is to pray. It is the first thing we should do after waking up early in the morning. Second, we need to listen to God's speaking; this is to read the Word. We should do this after praying. Third, we need to speak with our fellow Christians. This is to have fellowship with them, not only in the meetings but also in our daily living. Fourth, we need to speak to unbelievers. This is to preach the gospel, and it is something we should do in season and out of season.

THE ALTAR REMOVING
THE BARRIER BETWEEN MAN AND GOD,
ENABLING MAN TO COME NEAR TO GOD AGAIN

In the Old Testament we can see a picture of man's fellowship with God. This picture is the picture of man going to the altar to draw near to God. In the Old Testament time the altar of God was where God was. If a man wanted to come to God, he had to come to the altar of God. Hence, only those who went to the altar were able to meet God.

The Bible often uses prophecies and types to speak about God's salvation. The altar is a type of the cross that removes the barrier between man and God so that man may draw near to God. The Pentateuch, written by Moses, contains many descriptions of the altar that describe how a person should approach God. However, the records in the Pentateuch mainly emphasize the facts and not so much the feeling and taste concerning the altar. Most pleasant things taste sweet, and this sweet taste is closely related to man's emotions. In the Psalms some of the experienced ones expressed the sweet taste of their experiences of the altar. For example, Psalm 43:4a says, "And I will go to the altar of God, / To God my exceeding joy." When man comes to the altar, he comes to the God of exceeding joy. In Psalm 84 the sons of Korah also described their feeling about the altar, saying, "At Your two altars even the sparrow has found a home; / And the swallow, a nest for herself, / Where she may lay her young, / O Jehovah of hosts, my King and my God" (v. 3).

In the book of Numbers, Korah and his followers rebelled against God and received a very severe judgment. Because they rebelled to the uttermost, the judgment they received was the most severe the human race had seen (Num. 16). This group of people had been displeasing to God, yet when their descendants wrote psalms, they were able to fellowship with God with a heart devoid of fear, and they became those who longed after God. This was possible because of the altar, which removes the barrier and the distance between man and God. The description of the psalmist's feeling about the altar in Psalm 84:3-4 is the most beautiful, the fullest, and the highest in the entire Bible. While considering the habitation of God, the psalmist thought of the altar and expressed his feeling concerning it with poetic expressions. As a descendant of a rebel, he had been far off from God, yet now he could draw near to God because of the altar. Therefore, because he was unable to express his inner feeling with ordinary words, he used the sparrow and the swallow as illustrations.

Psalm 102:7 says, "I watch, and I am like / A lone sparrow on a housetop." Here it says that the sparrow is lonely and in affliction, yet it is watchful before God. This shows us that in the Psalms the sparrow refers to a person who lives in the presence of God. The sparrows mentioned in Matthew 10:29 and 31 show us that although a sparrow is worthless in itself, it is precious in the sight of God. Therefore, the sparrows in Matthew 10 also refer to those who live in the presence of God.

Jeremiah 8:6-7 says, "I have listened carefully and heard; / They have not spoken rightly; / There is no one who repents of his wickedness, / Saying, What have I done? / Everyone turns to his own course, / Like a horse rushing headlong into battle. / Even the stork in the sky / Knows its appointed times, / And the turtledove and the swallow and the crane / Keep the time of their coming; / But my people do not know the ordinance of Jehovah." The people of God turn to their own course instead of to God. The stork in the sky knows its appointed times, and the turtledove and the swallow keep the time of their coming, but God's people do not know the ordinance of God. The swallow here also signifies the people of God. Therefore, like the sparrow and the swallow, the people of God should know the ordinance of God, the time of God, and should live in His presence.

THOSE WHO COME TO THE ALTAR
BEING THE WEAK ONES

The sparrow and the swallow, being small, are very weak. This indicates that the psalmist felt his own frailty and insignificance. Everyone who has truly met God feels very small. All those who come to God through the cross also feel very small. Whoever feels that he is great has no way to come to the cross, and the altar is useless to him.

THOSE WHO COME TO THE ALTAR
BEING THE HELPLESS ONES

The sparrow and the swallow are not only small but also

without a definite dwelling place and safeguard. Furthermore, they have nothing to turn to or rely on. This was another feeling the psalmist had. He felt that in this universe he had no one to turn to or rely on. He could only find rest and joy at the altar. Everyone who comes to the cross has the sense that in the universe he has no one whom he can trust and on whom he can rely. If a person feels that he has someone or something to depend on, then the cross has lost its place in him. He has lost the real taste and feeling of the cross. Most of the time people experience the cross not when they are restful but when they are feeling completely helpless. Psalm 102 shows us this in the situation of the sparrow. Brought by God into a situation of helplessness, the sparrow waits for God in the night.

THE ALTAR BEING THE REAL RESTING PLACE OF A CHRISTIAN

The psalmist felt that at the altar he had a resting place, just like a swallow finding a nest where she can lay her young. According to the psalmist's feeling, the altar—typifying the Lord's cross, which took away man's sins and removed all the problems between man and God, thereby enabling God to gain man—is a place of rest to those who come to God. On the earth our real rest and satisfaction is our experience of the cross. When we experience the cross, the cross becomes our place of rest. Therefore, the work of the cross in dealing with sins, in consecration, and in breaking us is altogether for us to gain satisfaction and rest so that we may have a sense of sweetness. This is the true rest of a Christian.

THE ALTAR BEING THE PLACE FOR THE MULTIPLICATION OF THE SPIRITUAL LIFE

The emphasis of the sparrow is on its helplessness and worthlessness. The emphasis of the swallow is on her laying her young in the nest. This is a type of our caring for those who are younger than we are for the multiplication of life. In chapter one of the Song of Songs the Lord tells those who follow Him not to forget to pasture their young goats by the shepherds' tents (v. 8b). This also corresponds to Psalm 84, which says that not only do we ourselves find rest at the altar, but we can also "lay our young" there for the multiplication of our spiritual life. Through the preaching of the gospel we must "lay our young" by bringing sinners to the cross of Christ to produce spiritual children.

Psalm 84:4 says, "Blessed are those who dwell in Your house." Verse three speaks about the altar, and verse four speaks about the house of Jehovah. This means that only those who come to the altar can come into the house of Jehovah.

THE ALTAR BEING THE CROSS
IN THE NEW TESTAMENT

The altar is the cross in the New Testament. Only those who know the cross can know God. Regrettably, many people do not have a sufficiently clear knowledge of the cross. Thus, their contact with God is not very deep. The cross accomplished several things. First, it dealt with man's sins. Second, it dealt with all persons, things, and matters. Third, it dealt with our very being so that God could gain our entire being.

Everyone who has passed through the work of the cross will experience two results. On the one hand, he will have a place of rest. The place of rest for a Christian is in his experience of the cross. On the other hand, he will bear fruit. Psalm 84:3 shows us that not only does the sparrow find a resting place at the altar, but the swallow also finds a nest there where she may lay her young. John 15 shows us that in order to bear fruit the branches must pass through the cross. Without the experience of the cross, there will be no fruit. The unfruitful Christian will suffer a great loss before God, because the Lord said that every branch that does not bear fruit shall be taken away (v. 2). This is very serious.

HOW CHRISTIANS BEAR FRUIT

Psalm 84 and John 15 are connected. Psalm 84 uses animals to signify Christians, showing how we are like the sparrow and the swallow, worthless and useless. Real Christians are just like this in the eyes of the world, having no attractive form or beauty and without ability or education. They are small and worthless. However, all those who come to the altar have to be small. Without being small, one cannot come to the altar. John 15 uses a plant to symbolize Christians, showing that we are just like the branches of a vine, which are not fit for use as lumber. Thus, they appear to be useless. Also, the period of time during which they blossom is so short that their flowers are hardly seen. As branches of the vine, we have no other use except to bear fruit.

Therefore, Christians are useless in the eyes of the world. They have no other use besides the overflowing of life. Although Christians are very small and worthless in the eyes of the world, they can lay their young like the swallow in Psalm 84. They can propagate the spiritual life. Christians who have experienced the cross are like this. They seem to be useless, yet they can produce other Christians. It is just like the branches of the vine in John 15. Every branch that does not bear fruit shall be taken away, but those that bear fruit express the life of the vine.

EXPERIENCING THE CROSS BY BEING JOINED
TO THE LORD'S RESURRECTION POWER

Psalm 84:4 speaks about dwelling in the house of God to fellowship with Him. John 15 speaks of abiding in the Lord to fellowship with Him. The Lord, Christ, is the house of God. Hence, to dwell in the Lord is to dwell in the house of God. Psalm 84 speaks about the altar, that is, the experience of the cross. John 15 says that the branches have to abide in the vine, emphasizing our union with the Lord. These are the two ends of our spiritual experience, which is the most precious experience in the Christian life. Union with the Lord cannot be separated from the experience of the cross. True union with the Lord requires a real experience of the cross. If we want to have the real experience of the cross, we must be joined to the Lord in His resurrection power.

To know the power of resurrection, we need to love the experience of the cross. In the New Testament God does not look at a person's children in the flesh. Rather, God looks at a Christian's spiritual children. On the spiritual side, if a Christian does not have any children, this means that he is barren. This is a most shameful thing. Psalm 1 says that a person who fears God is like a tree that yields its fruit in its season (v. 3). Revelation 22 also says that in the New Jerusalem the tree of life yields its fruit each month (v. 2). What God regards as important is fruit-bearing, that is, the multiplication of life. John 15 shows us that our abiding in the Lord and the Lord's abiding in us is for fruit-bearing. If we do not bear fruit, then we surely have a problem. We may feel that we are all right and that our prayers are effective. However, if we do not have fruit, this indicates that there is something wrong with us. The Lord said to Peter, "Do you love Me?...Feed My sheep" (John 21:17). In the Song of Songs, the Lord also told His pursuer, "Pasture your young goats / By the shepherds' tents" (1:8). Everyone who loves the Lord has young goats under his shepherding.

A person who wants to bear fruit must on the one hand have fellowship with the Lord to be filled with the Lord's life by receiving His abundant life. On the other hand, he must have the experience of the cross and be broken so that he can flow out the Lord's life. Without being broken, he cannot have the overflow of life. This is a principle. Some people have much prayer and fellowship with the Lord, yet they have no fruit. This is because they have not been broken. Paul told the Galatians, "My children, with whom I travail again in birth until Christ is formed in you " (Gal. 4:19). If a person is not broken, he cannot have any fruit. A person who has been broken is like water, having no form of his own. No matter where he is, he can adjust. Wherever he is, he can flow in and also flow out life.

ABOUT THE AUTHOR

Witness Lee was born in 1905 in northern China and raised in a Christian family. At age 19 he was fully captured for Christ and immediately consecrated himself to preach the gospel for the rest of his life. Early in his service, he met Watchman Nee, a renowned preacher, teacher, and writer. Witness Lee labored together with Watchman Nee under his direction. In 1934 Watchman Nee entrusted Witness Lee with the responsibility for his publication operation, called the Shanghai Gospel Bookroom.

Prior to the Communist takeover in 1949, Witness Lee was sent by Watchman Nee and his other co-workers to Taiwan to insure that the things delivered to them by the Lord would not be lost. Watchman Nee instructed Witness Lee to continue the former's publishing operation abroad as the Taiwan Gospel Bookroom, which has been publicly recognized as the publisher of Watchman Nee's works outside China. Witness Lee's work in Taiwan manifested the Lord's abundant blessing. From a mere 350 believers, newly fled from the mainland, the churches in Taiwan grew to 20,000 in five years.

In 1962 Witness Lee felt led of the Lord to come to the United States, settling in California. During his 35 years of service in the U.S., he ministered in weekly meetings and weekend conferences, delivering several thousand spoken messages. Much of his speaking has since been published as over 400 titles. Many of these have been translated into over fourteen languages. He gave his last public conference in February 1997 at the age of 91.

He leaves behind a prolific presentation of the truth in the Bible. His major work, *Life-study of the Bible,* comprises over 25,000 pages of commentary on every book of the Bible from the perspective of the believers' enjoyment and experience of God's divine life in Christ through the Holy Spirit. Witness Lee was the chief editor of a new translation of the New Testament into Chinese called the Recovery Version and directed the translation of the same into English. The Recovery Version also appears in a number of other languages. He provided an extensive body of footnotes, outlines, and spiritual cross references. A radio broadcast of his messages can be heard on Christian radio stations in the United States. In 1965 Witness Lee founded Living Stream Ministry, a non-profit corporation, located in Anaheim, California, which officially presents his and Watchman Nee's ministry.

Witness Lee's ministry emphasizes the experience of Christ as life and the practical oneness of the believers as the Body of Christ. Stressing the importance of attending to both these matters, he led the churches under his care to grow in Christian life and function. He was unbending in his conviction that God's goal is not narrow sectarianism but the Body of Christ. In time, believers began to meet simply as the church in their localities in response to this conviction. In recent years a number of new churches have been raised up in Russia and in many eastern European countries.